CIVIC READINESS

The
Executive Branch

By Tracy Vonder Brink

Table of Contents

A Starfish Book

SEAHORSE PUBLISHING

Teaching Tips for Caregivers:

As a caregiver, you can help your child succeed in school by giving them a strong foundation in language and literacy skills and a desire to learn to read.

This book helps children grow by letting them practice reading skills.

Reading for pleasure and interest will help your child to develop reading skills and will give your child the opportunity to practice these skills in meaningful ways.

- Encourage your child to read on her own at home
- Encourage your child to practice reading aloud
- Encourage activities that require reading
- Establish a reading time
- Talk with your child
- Give your child writing materials

Teaching Tips for Teachers:

Research shows that one of the best ways for students to learn a new topic is to read about it.

Before Reading

- Read the "Words to Know" and discuss the meaning of each word.
- Read the back cover to see what the book is about.

During Reading

- When a student gets to a word that is unknown, ask them to look at the rest of the sentence to find clues to help with the meaning of the unknown word.
- Ask the student to write down any pages of the book that was confusing to them.

After Reading

- Discuss the main idea of the book.
- Ask students to give one detail that they learned in the book by showing a text dependent answer from the book.

The Executive Branch

The U.S. government has three **branches**.

The **executive** branch carries out **laws**.

The **president** is part of the executive branch.

The president is the top leader.

George Washington was the first president.

The president must be at least 35 years old.

The president approves new laws.

He or she leads the **armed forces**.

He or she meets with leaders of other countries.

Many people help the president.

The vice president may do the job if the president cannot.

Kamala Harris was the first woman to be vice president.

The president works with a group of people called the **Cabinet**.

The vice president and 15 leaders make up the Cabinet.

They guide the president.

The president may meet with the Cabinet every week.

The executive branch has many other parts.

Each does jobs that help the country.

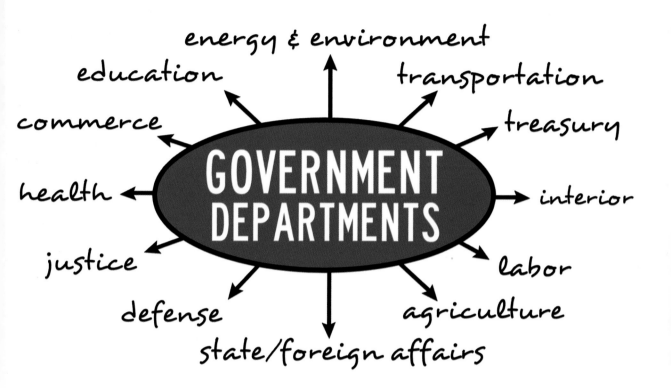

The Treasury prints new money every day.
It replaces old, worn-out money.

The Department of Defense protects the U.S.

The Department of Justice carries out laws.

It catches lawbreakers.

The Treasury takes care of the country's money.

It also prints the money we use.

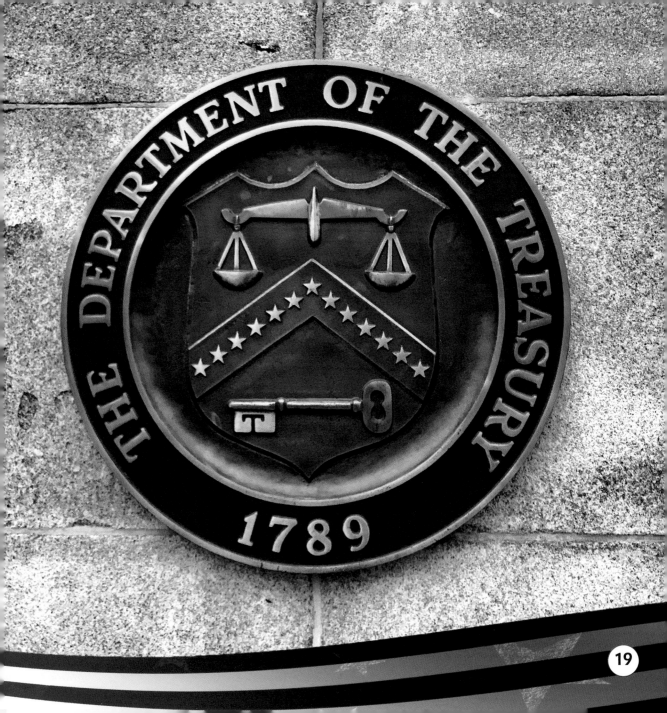

More than four million people work for the executive branch.

They work for our country every day.

Words to Know

armed forces (armd FOR-suhz): a country's military forces, especially its army, navy, and air force

branches (BRANCH-ez): main parts of a government

Cabinet (KAB-uh-nut): a group that gives advice to the president of the United States

executive (ug-ZEK-yoo-tive): the U.S. government branch that carries out laws

laws (lahwz): rules made by a government

president (PREZ-uh-dent): the head of the government in some countries, such as the United States

Index

Comprehension Questions

1. The top leader of the executive branch is _____.
    a. the president
    b. the vice president
    c. the judge

2. The first U.S. president was:
    a. Kamala Harris
    b. George Washington
    c. Donald Trump

3. Who takes care of the country's money?
    a. the Department of Defense
    b. the military
    c. the Treasury

4. **True or False:** The Department of Justice carries out laws.

5. **True or False:** The vice president leads the armed forces.

About the Author

Tracy Vonder Brink enjoys learning about the United States. She has visited the White House, where the president lives. She lives in Cincinnati with her husband, two daughters, and two rescue dogs.

Written by: Tracy Vonder Brink
Design by: Kathy Walsh
Editor: Kim Thompson

Library of Congress PCN Data
The Executive Branch / Tracy Vonder Brink
Civic Readiness
ISBN 978-1-63897-088-0 (hard cover)
ISBN 978-1-63897-174-0 (paperback)
ISBN 978-1-63897-260-0 (EPUB)
ISBN 978-1-63897-346-1 (eBook)
Library of Congress Control Number: 2021945253

Printed in the United States of America.

Photographs/Shutterstock: Cover ©Ken Wolter, ©Vertes Edmond Mihai, Cover & Pg 1©Castleski: Pg 4-21 © Lightspring: Pg 3 © Joseph Sohm: Pg 5 ©Hugo Brizard - YouGoPhoto: Pg 6 ©Black Creature 24: Pg 7 ©Evan El-Amin: Pg 9 ©Naresh777: Pg 11©mark reinstein: Pg 13 ©desdemona72: Pg 15 ©Bumble Dee: Pg 17©Mark Van Scyoc: Pg 19 ©DCStockPhotography: Pg 21 ©f11photo

Seahorse Publishing Company

www.seahorsepub.com

Published in the United States
Seahorse Publishing
PO Box 771325
Coral Springs, FL 33077